This Coloring Book Belongs To

_____

Copyright © 2021 by Rainbow House
Author, Illustrator - Shikha Nath

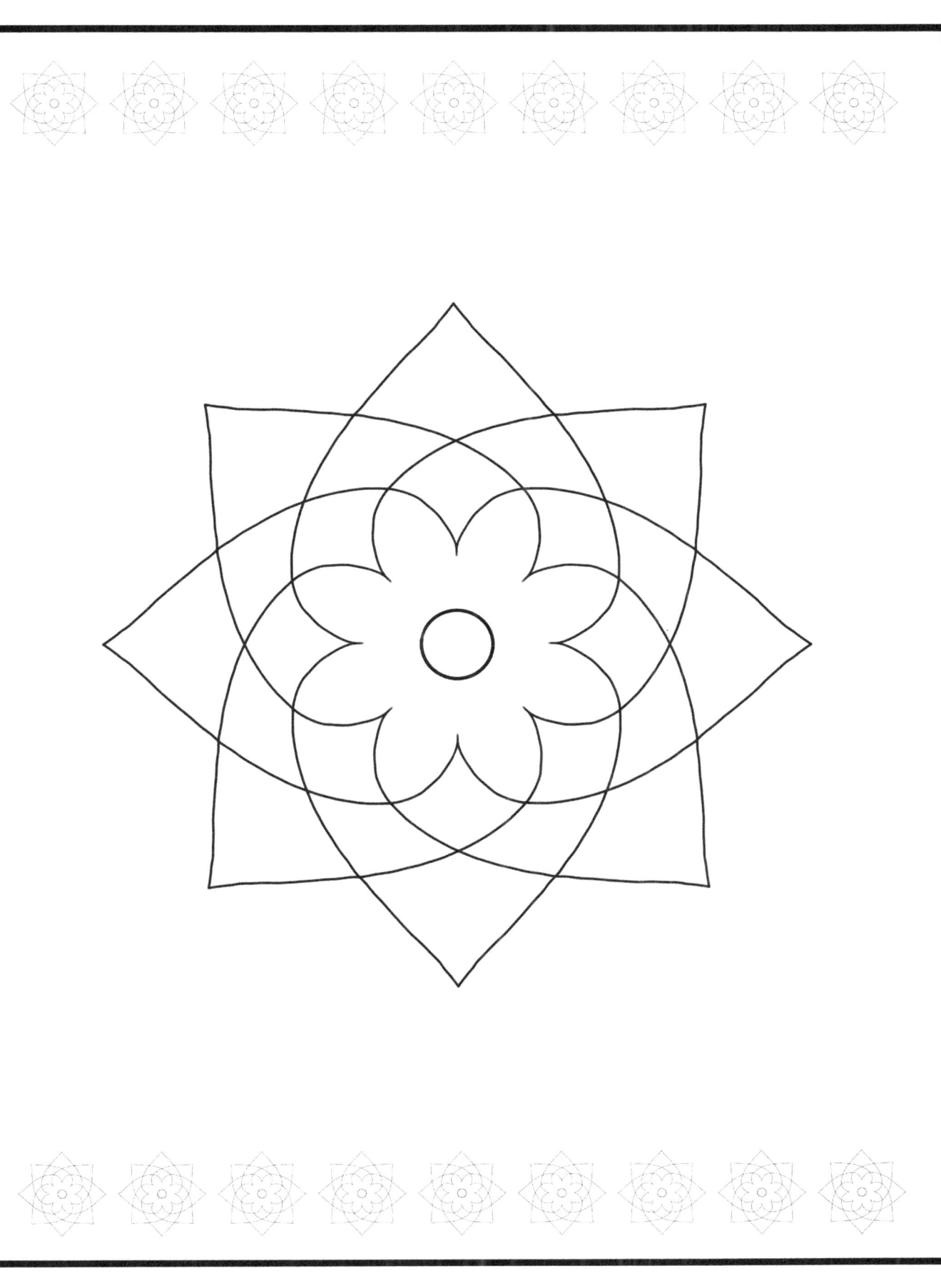

Let's be creative and start coloring our Awesome Mandalas!

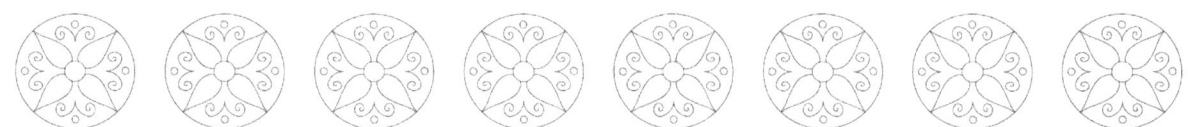

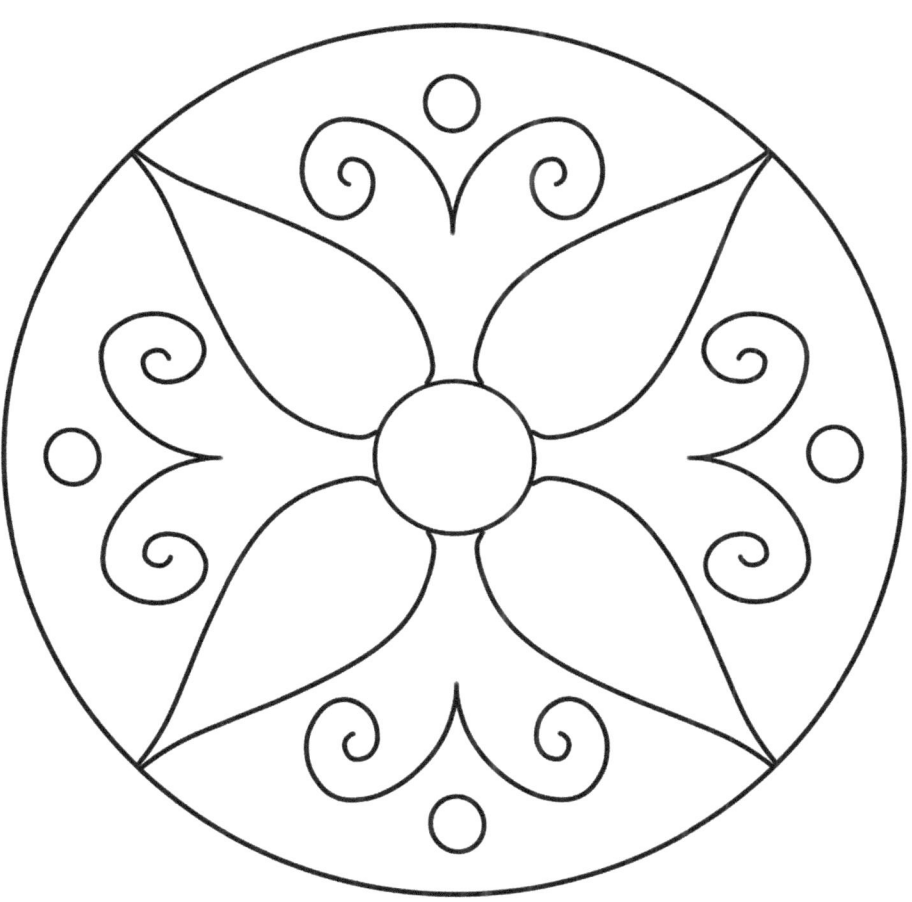

       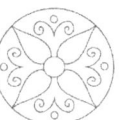

Q - Do you know what are the primary colors?

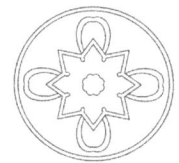     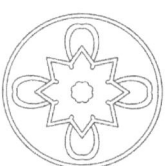

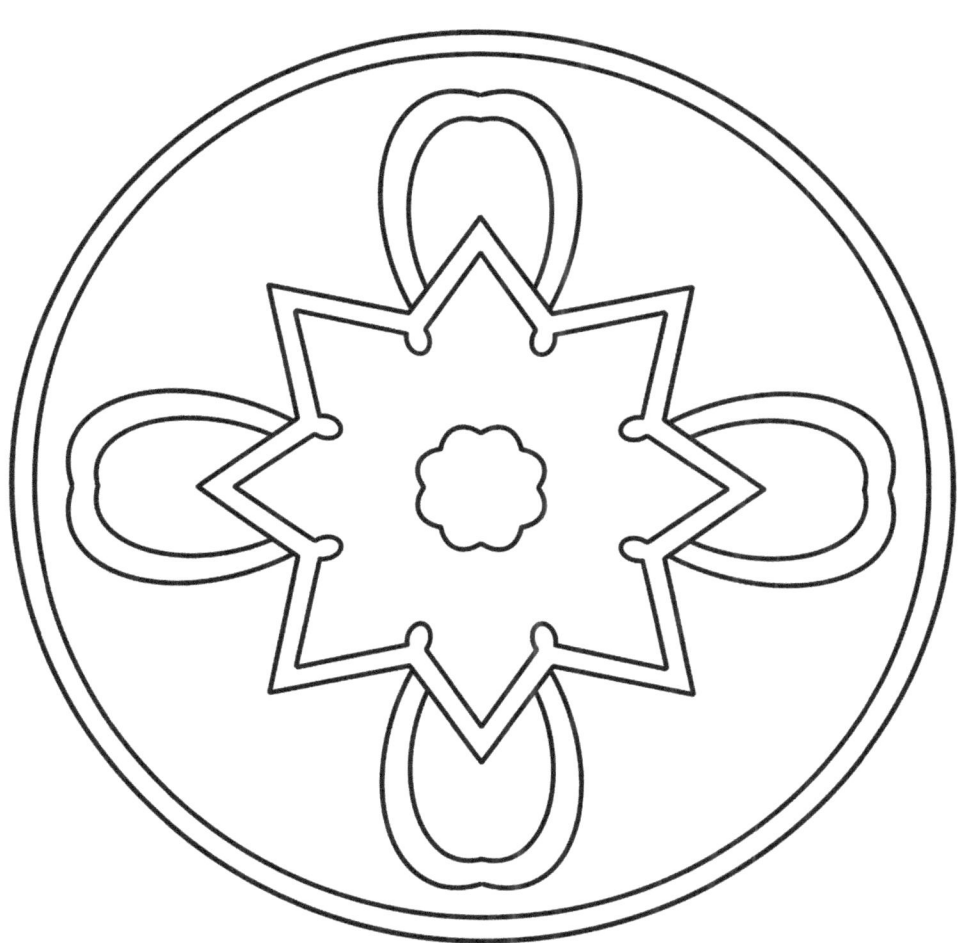

 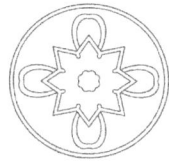 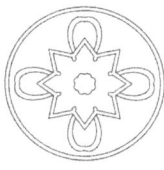   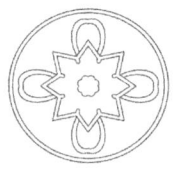

Ans - It's Red, Yellow and Blue!

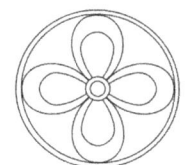 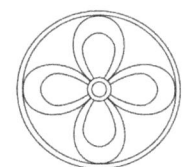 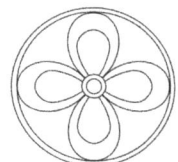 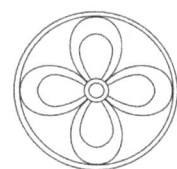 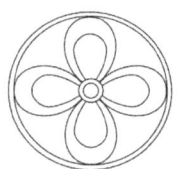

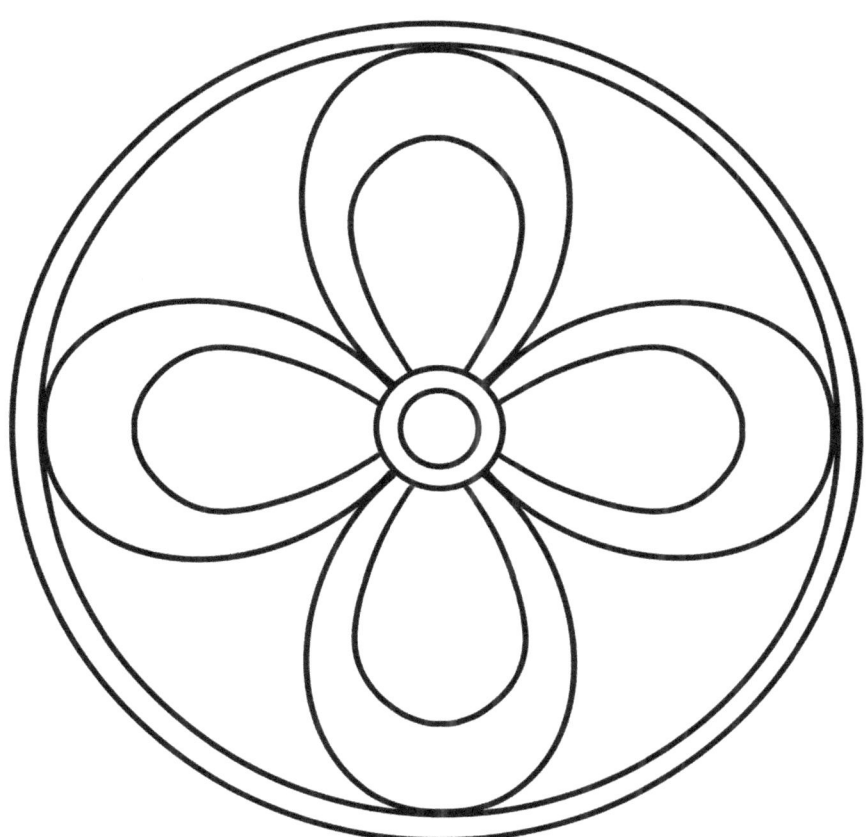

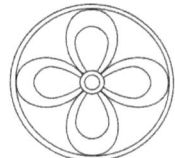 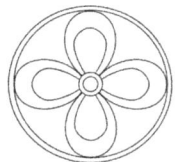 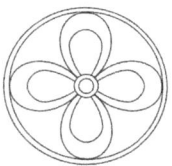 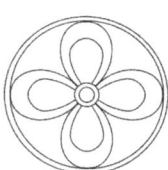 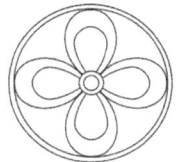

Q - Do you know How many months do we have in a year?

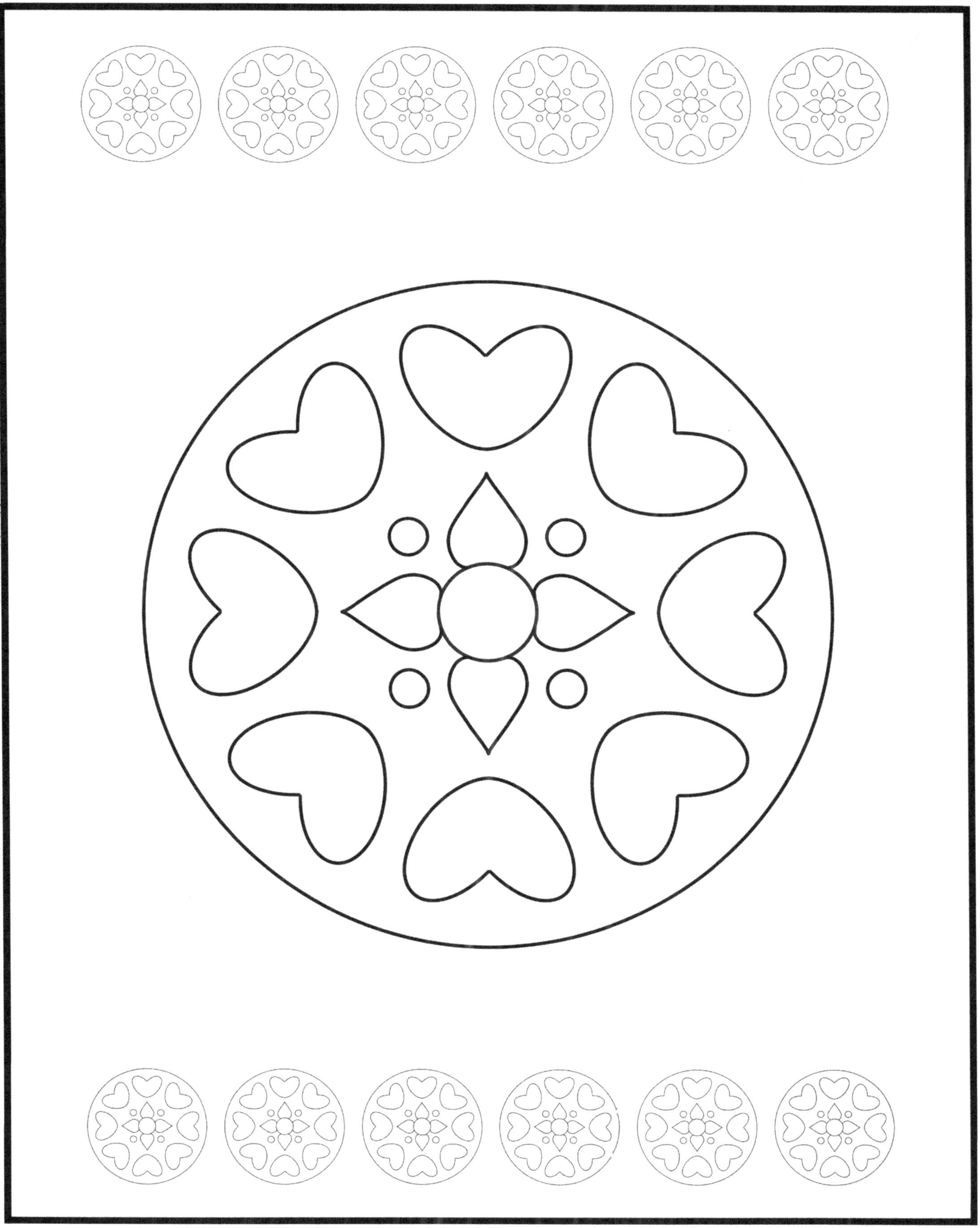

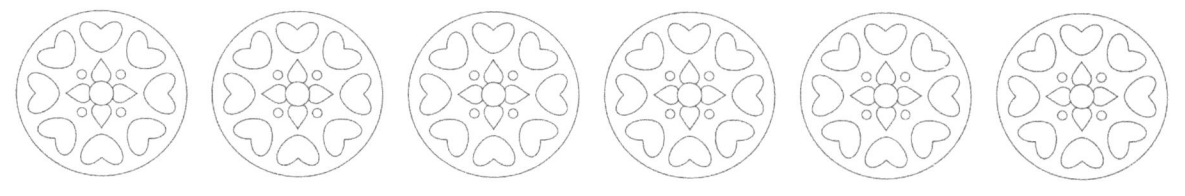

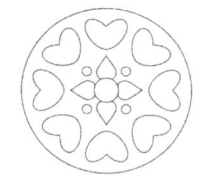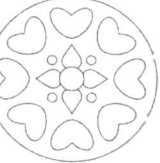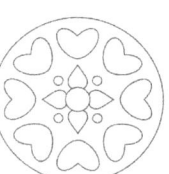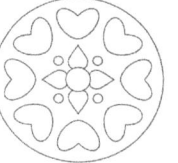

Ans - 12 Months!

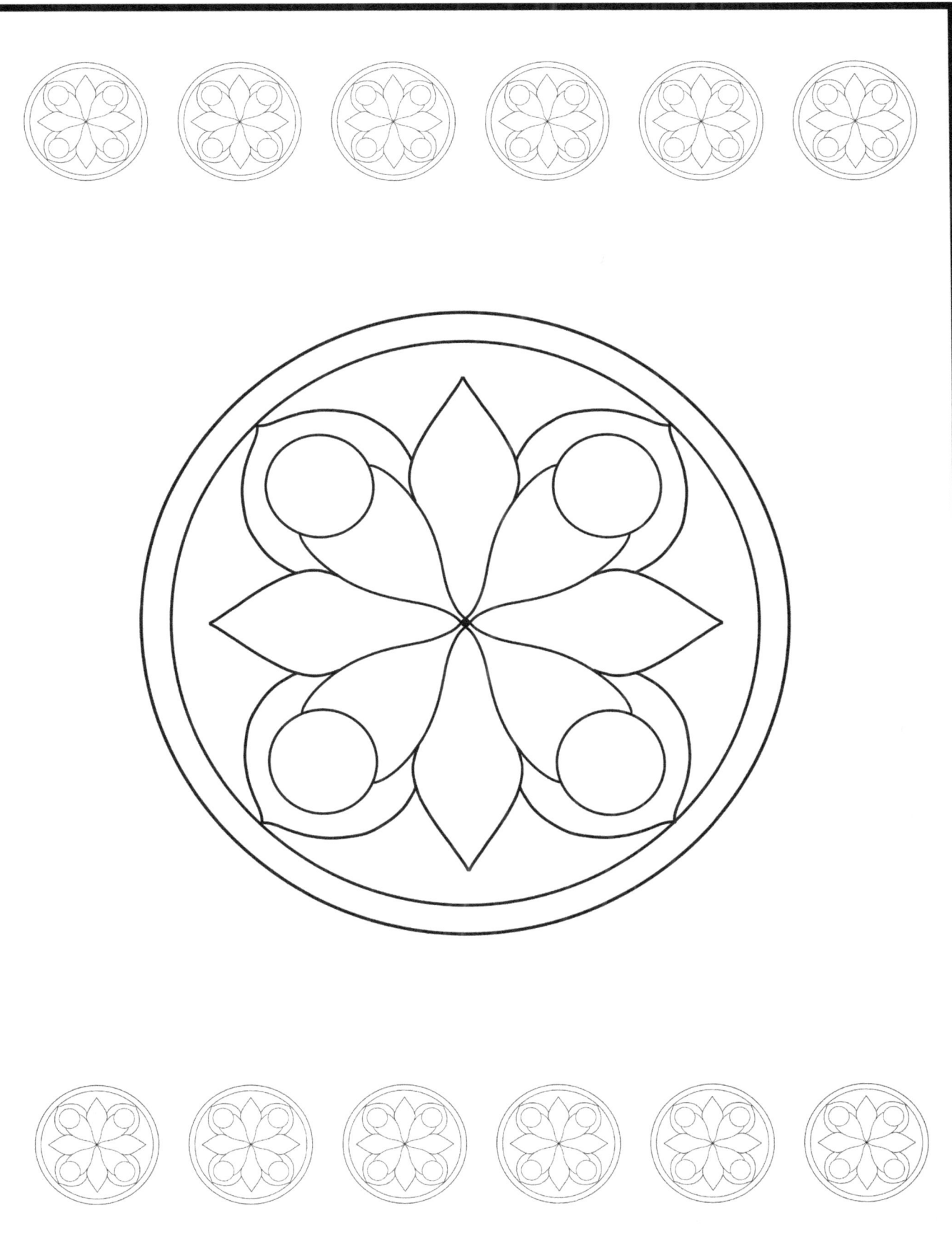

Q - How many days do we have in a week?

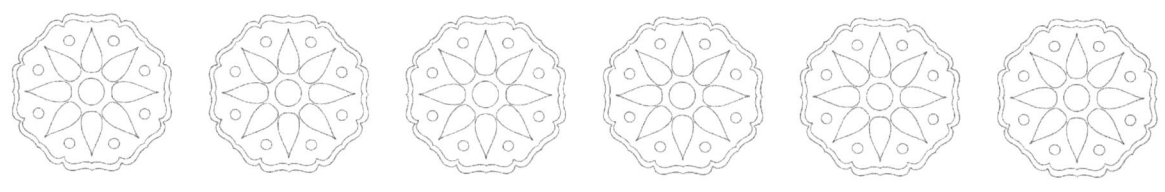
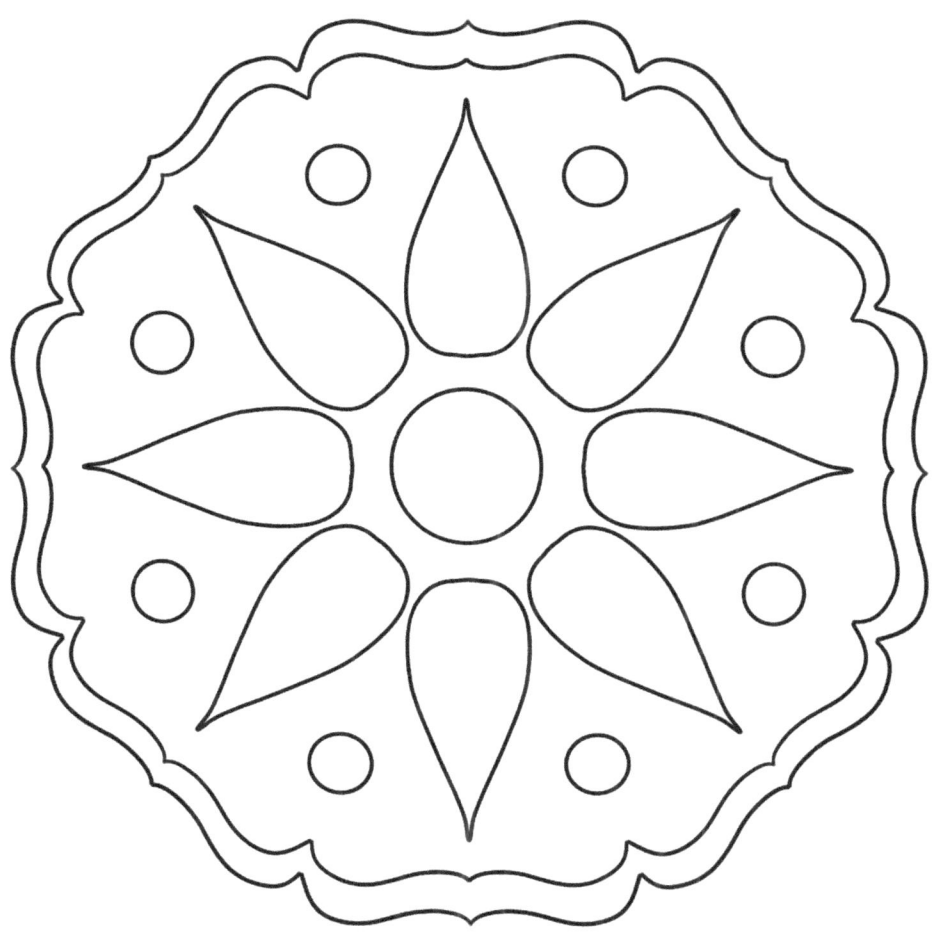
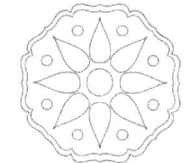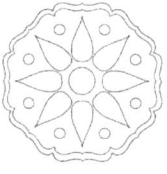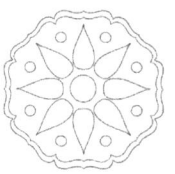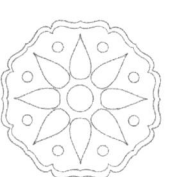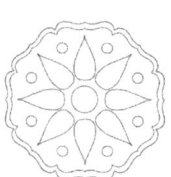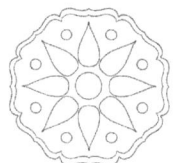

Ans - 7 Days!

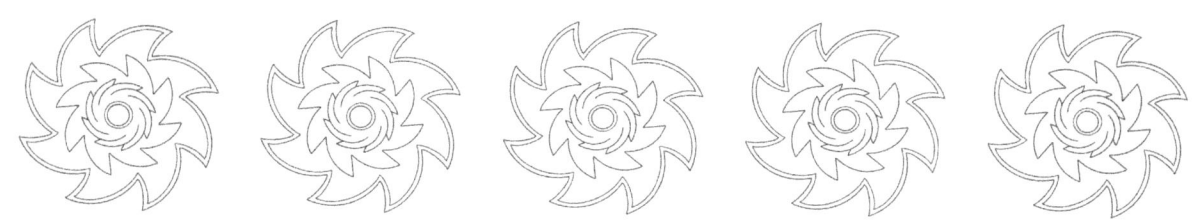
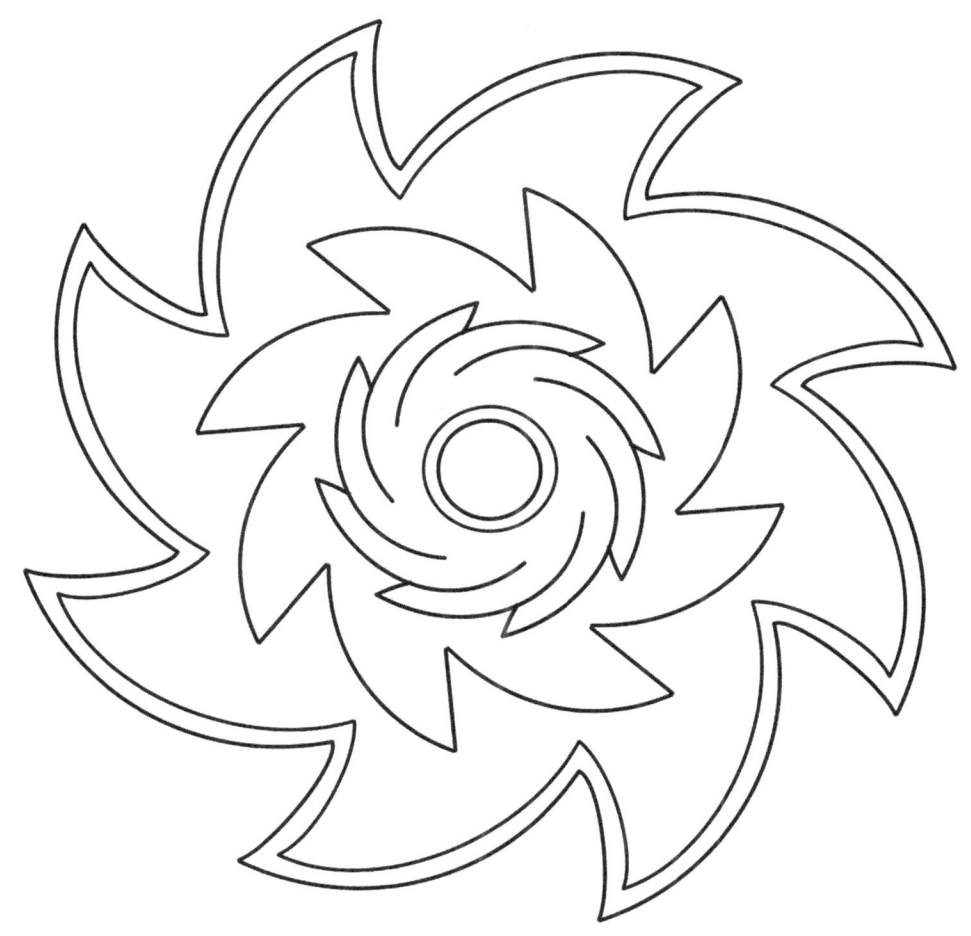
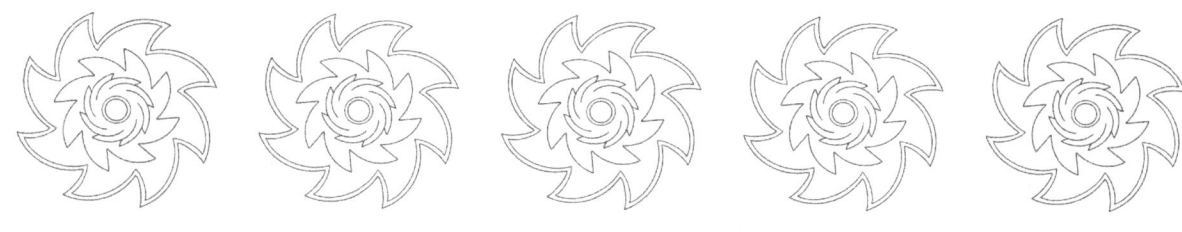

Q - How many days are there in a year?

Ans - 365 Days!

Q - What is 2+2?

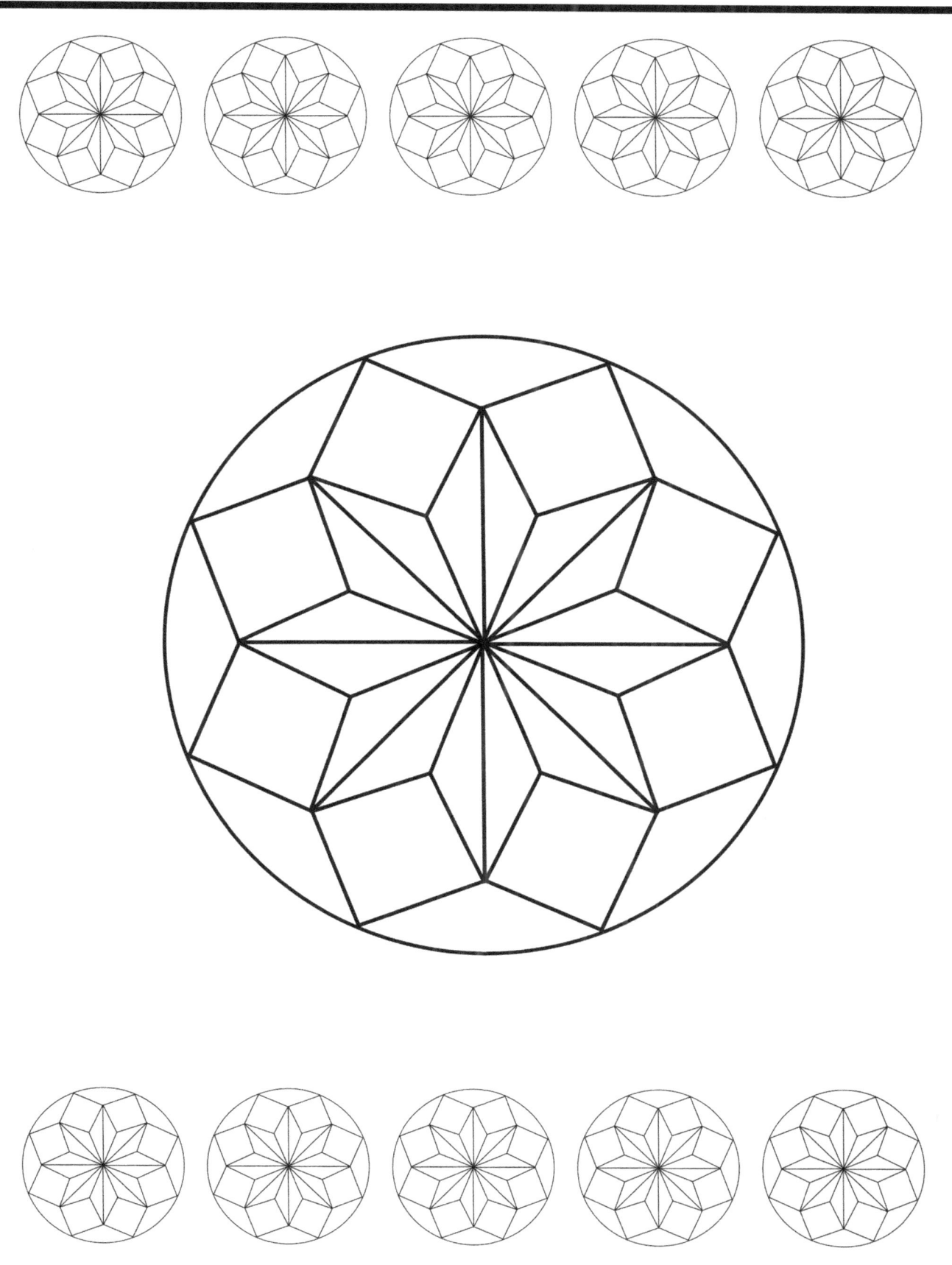

Ans - 4!

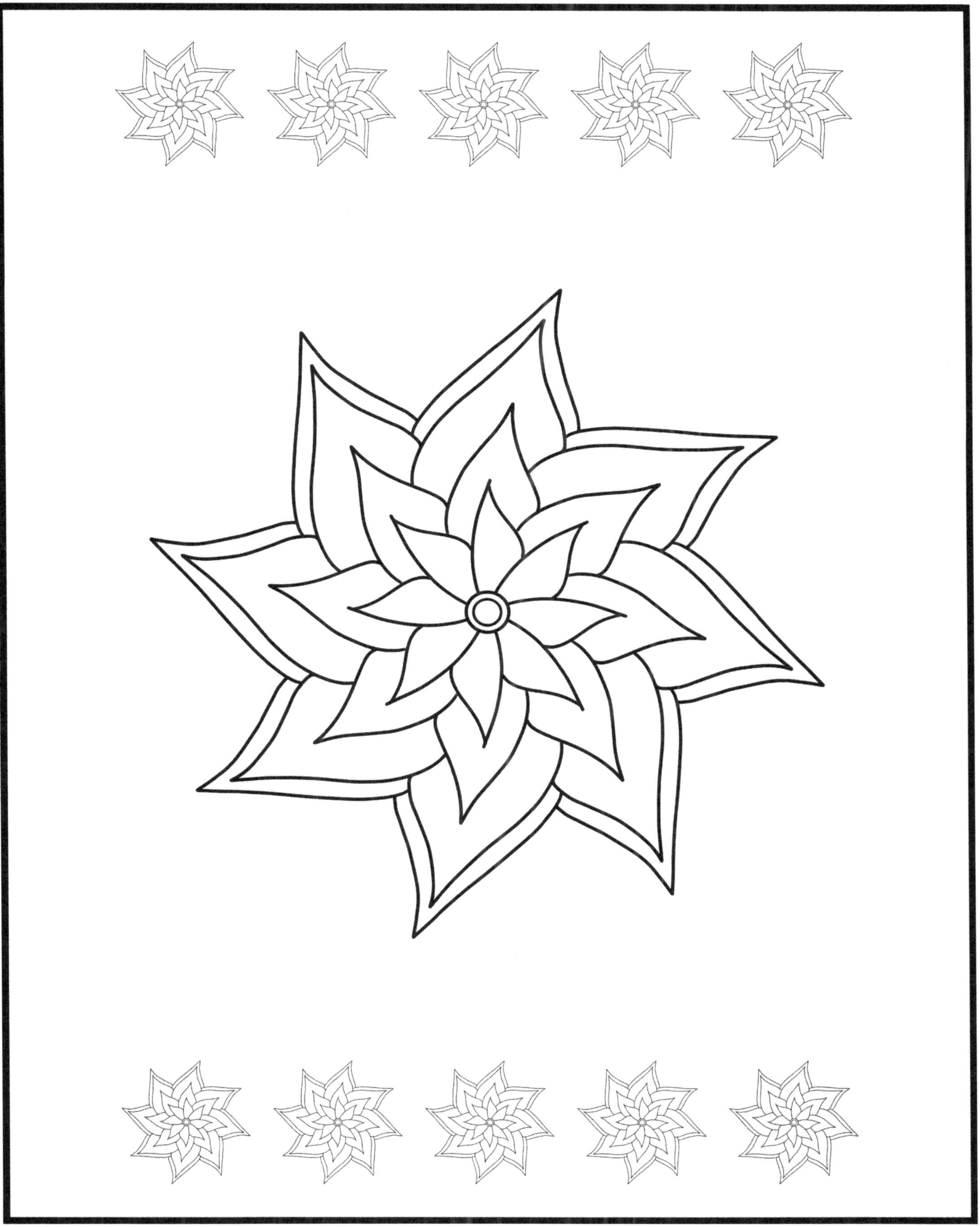

Q - Which number comes after 6?

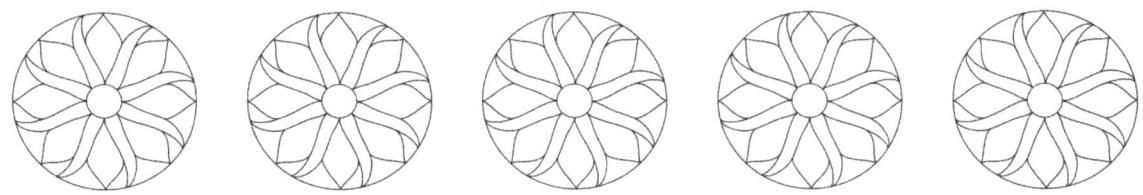
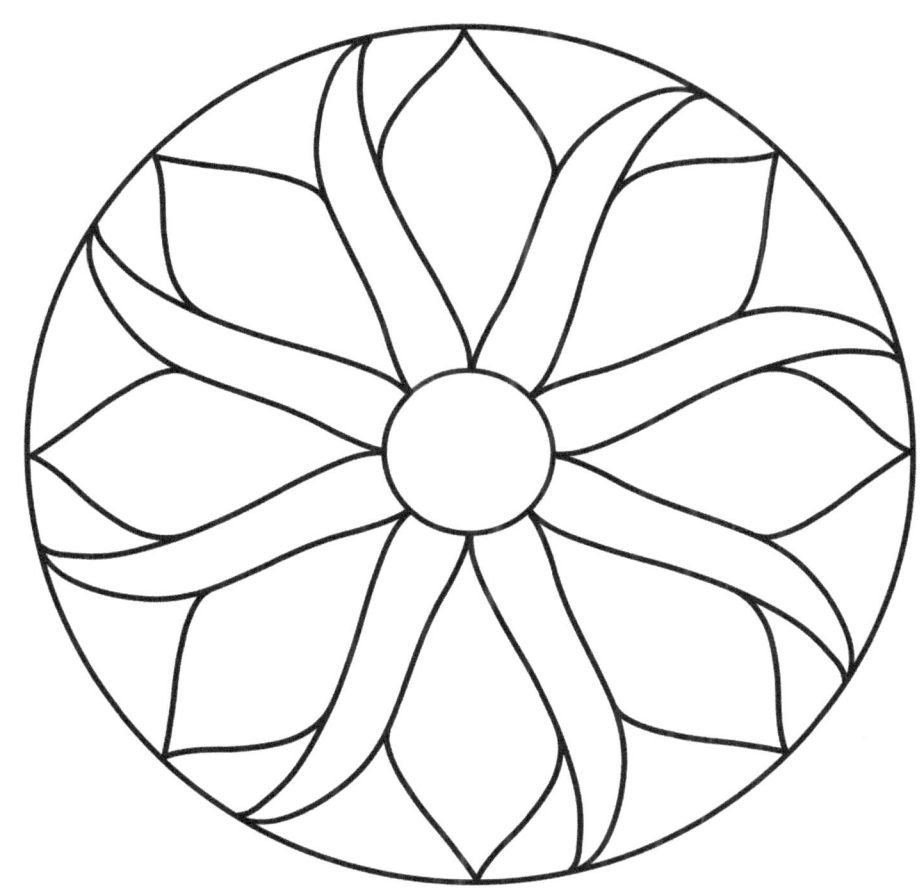
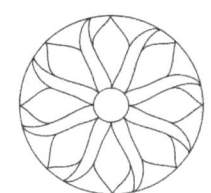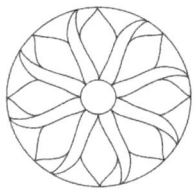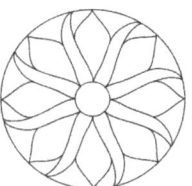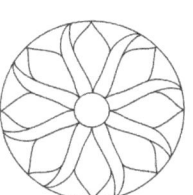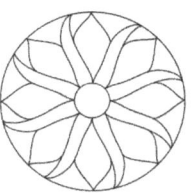

Ans - 7!

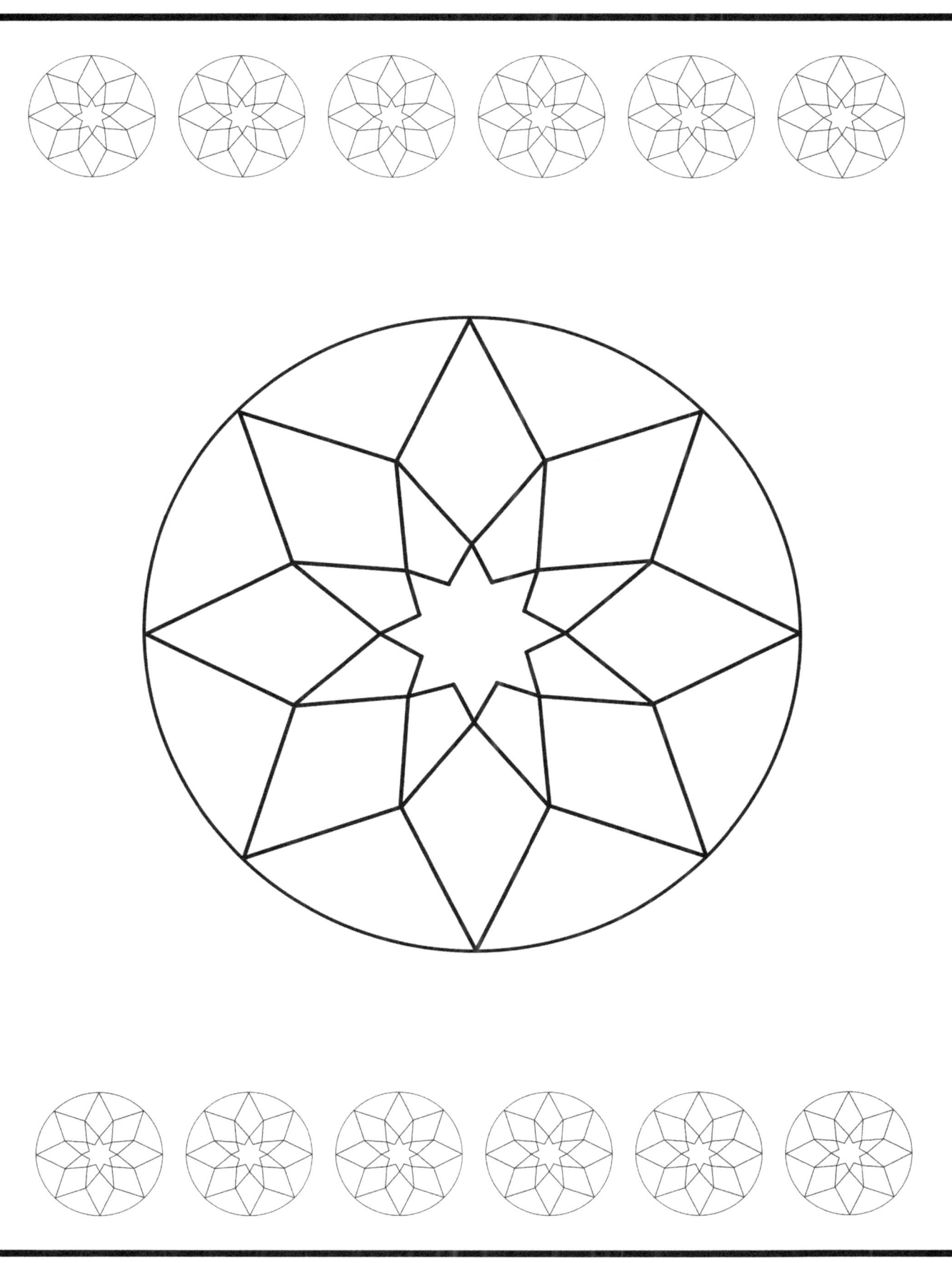

Q - How many colors are there in a rainbow?

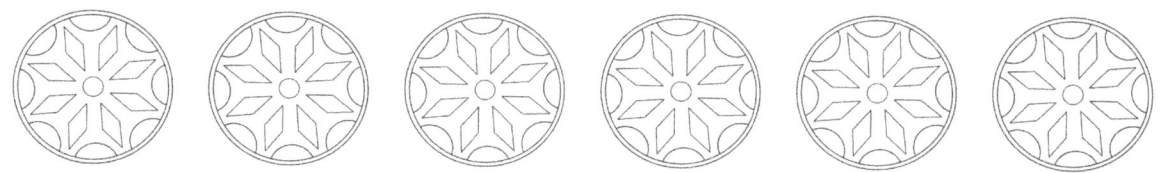
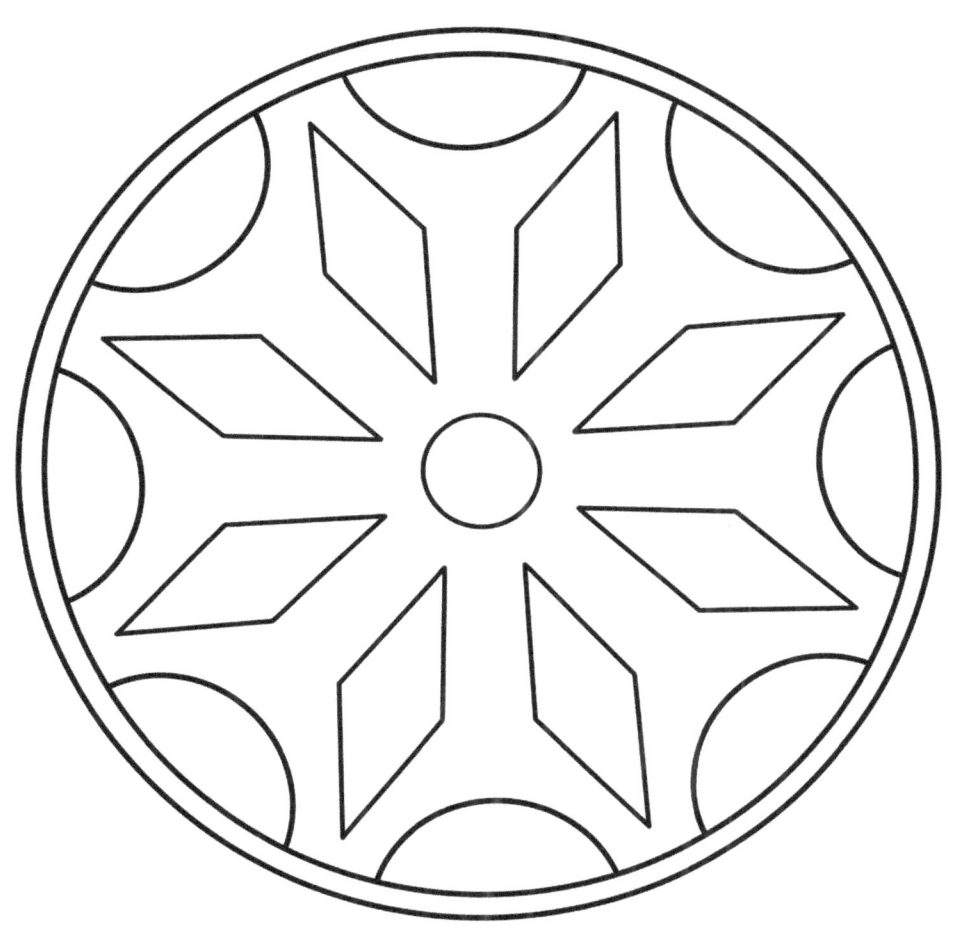
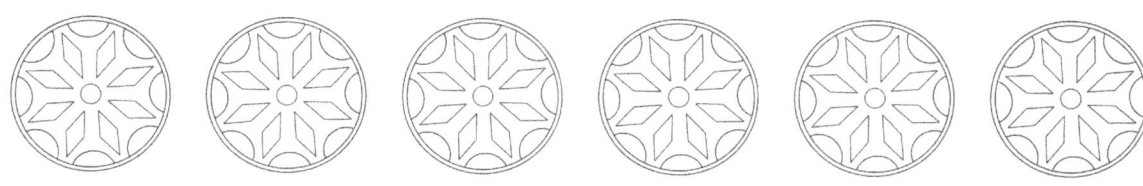

Ans - 7!

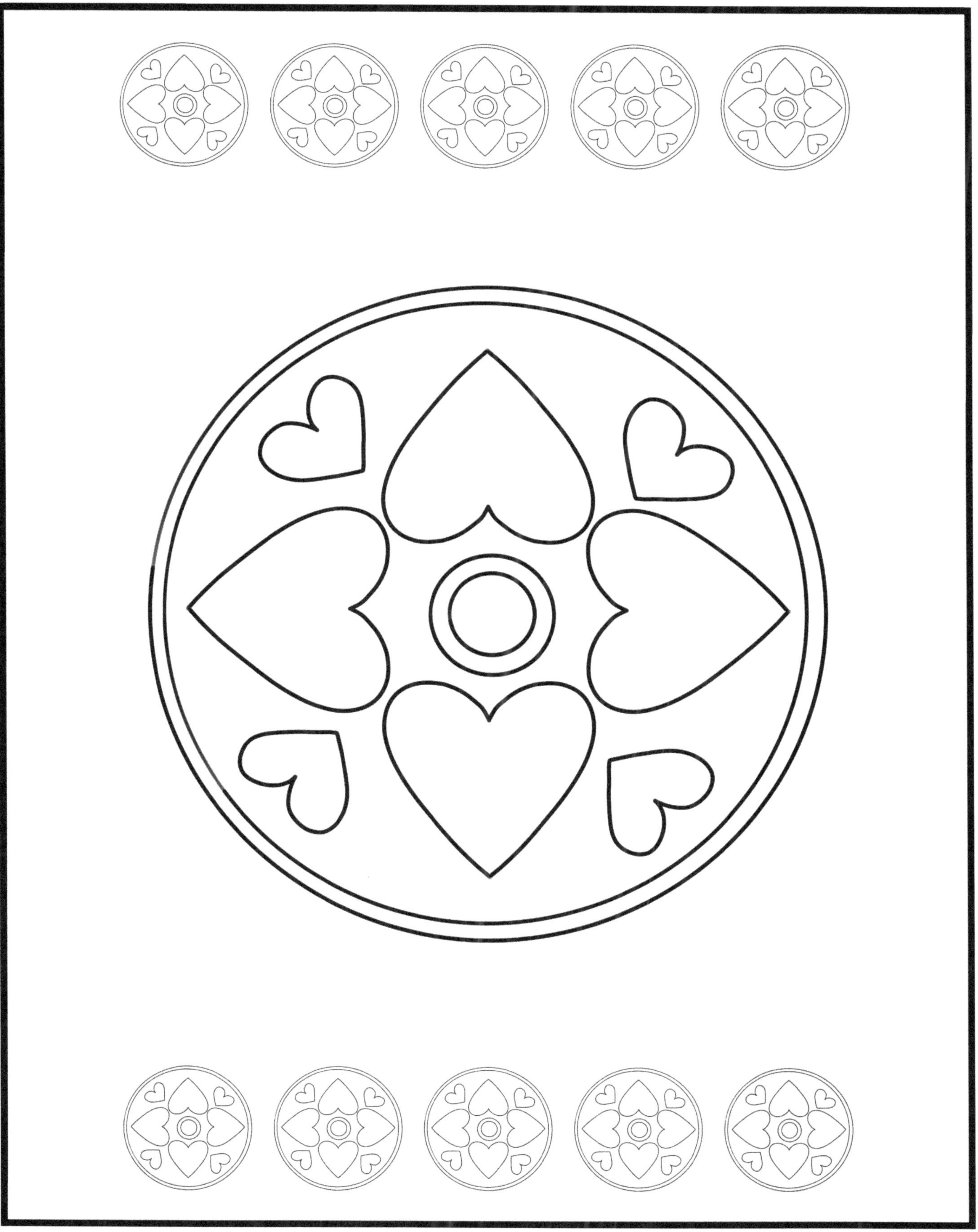

 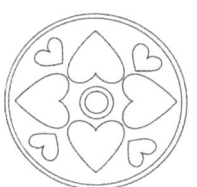  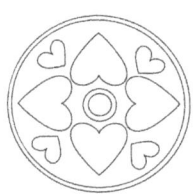 
 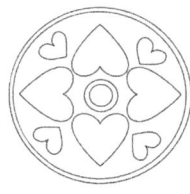  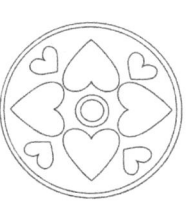 

Q - What are your ears for?

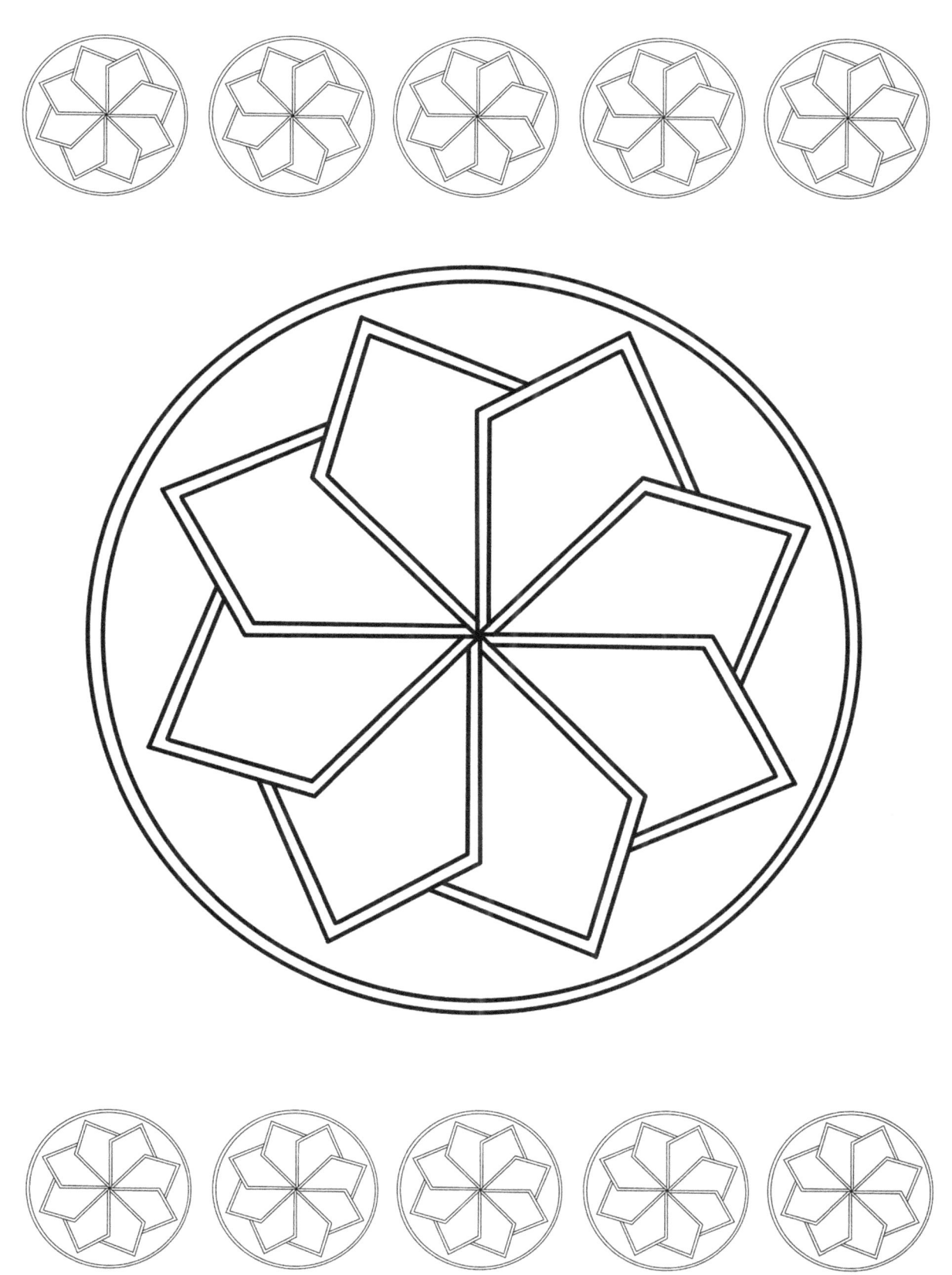

Ans - Listening/hearing!

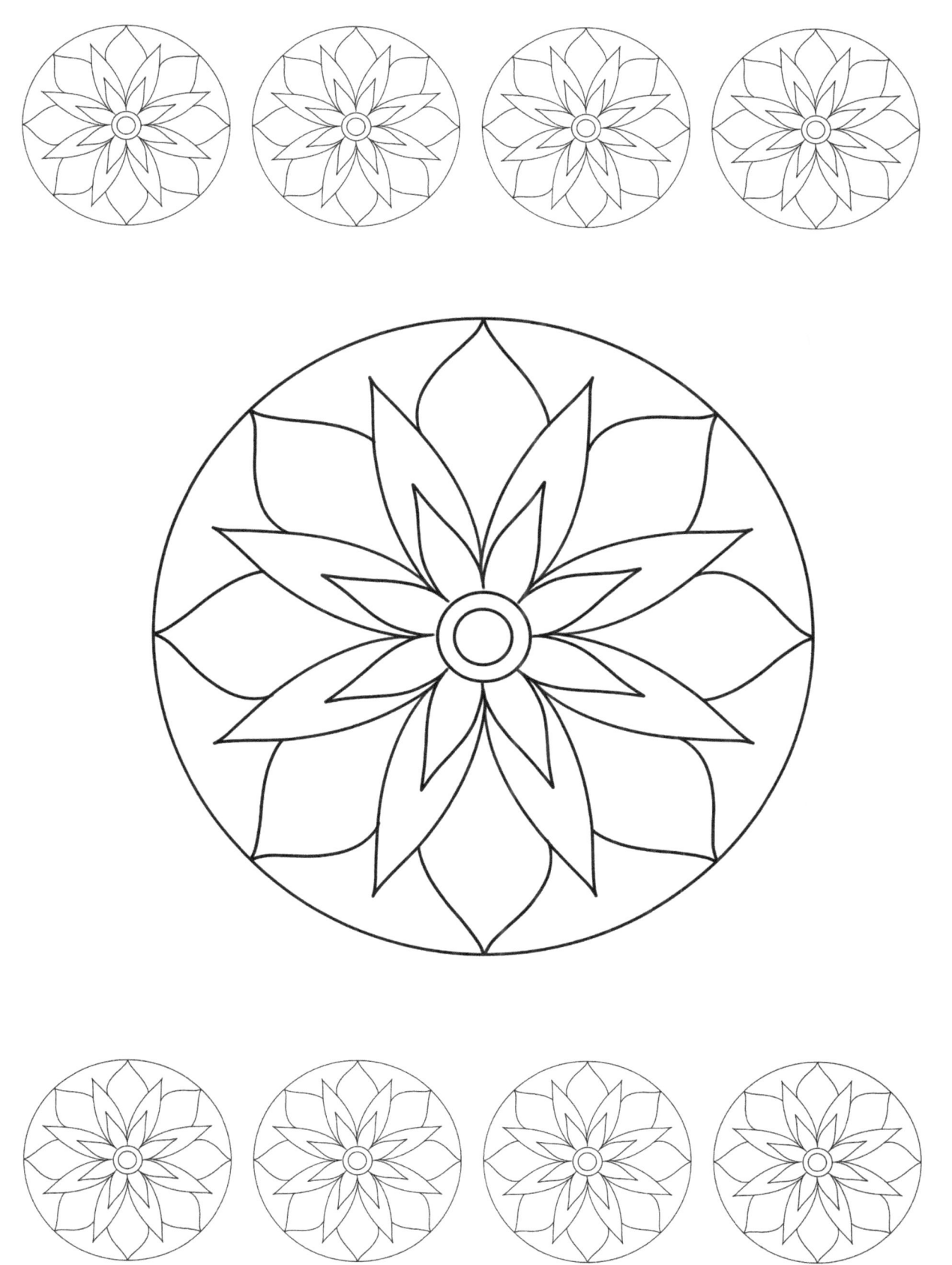

Q - Which day comes after Friday?

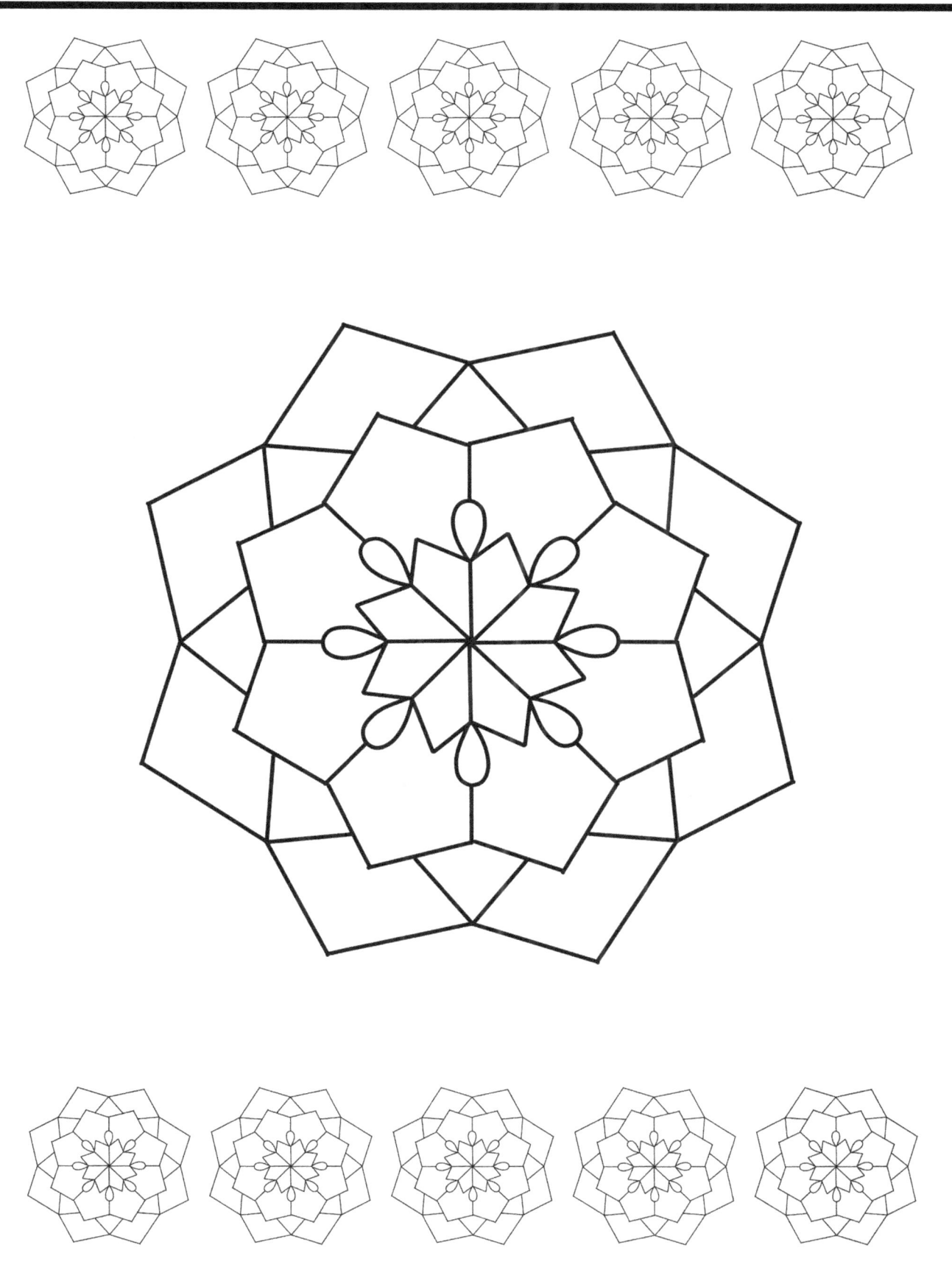

Ans - Saturday!

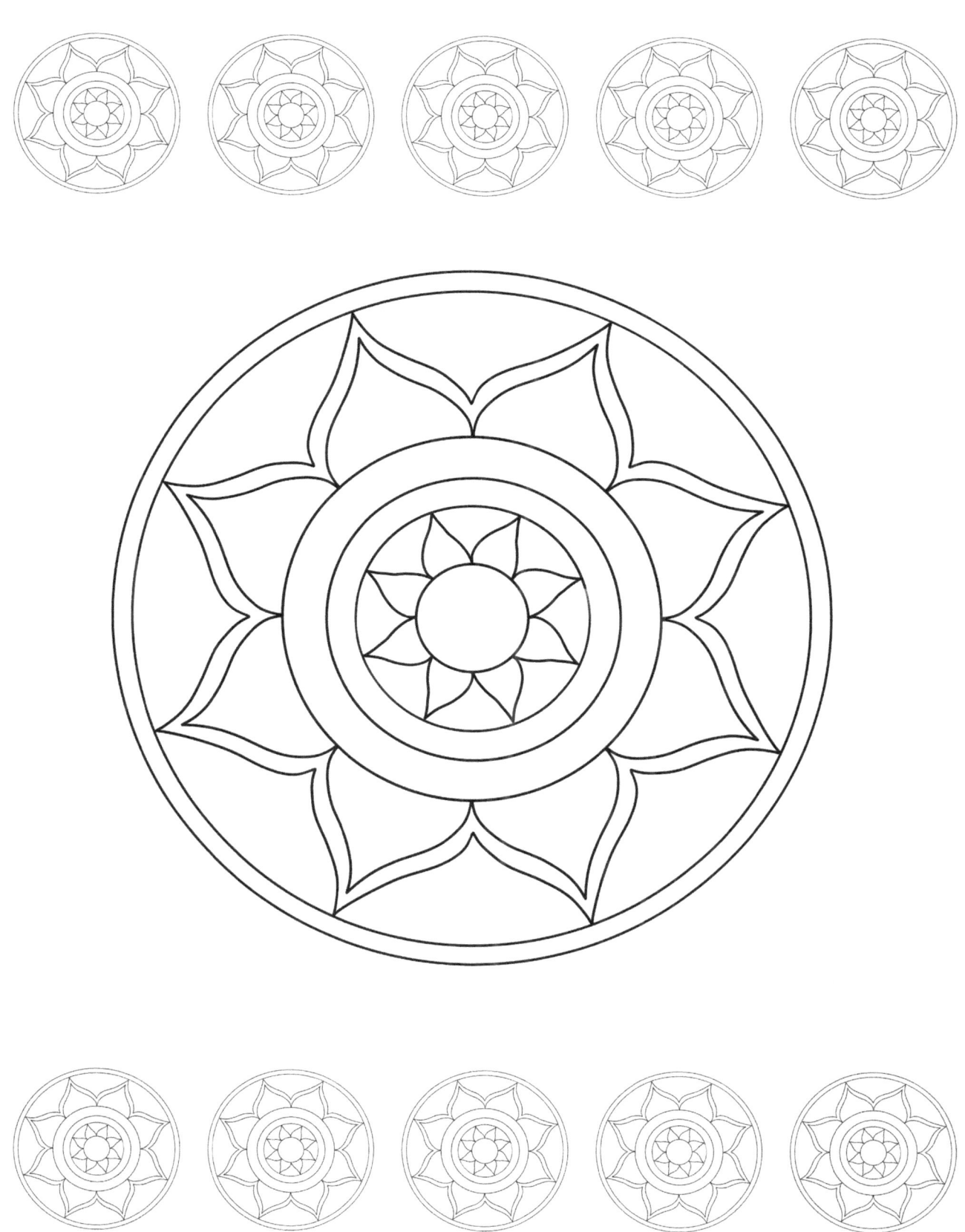

Q - We use our eyes to — see, hear, feel, eat?

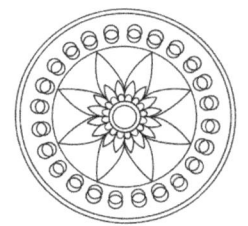 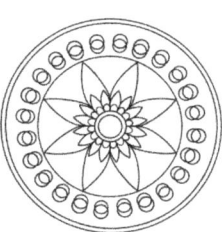 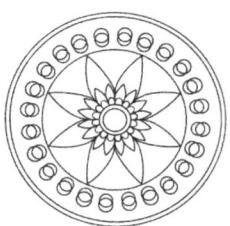 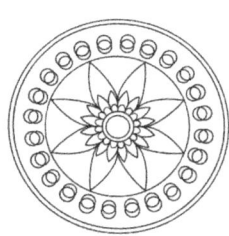 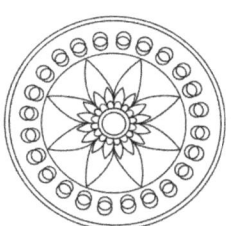

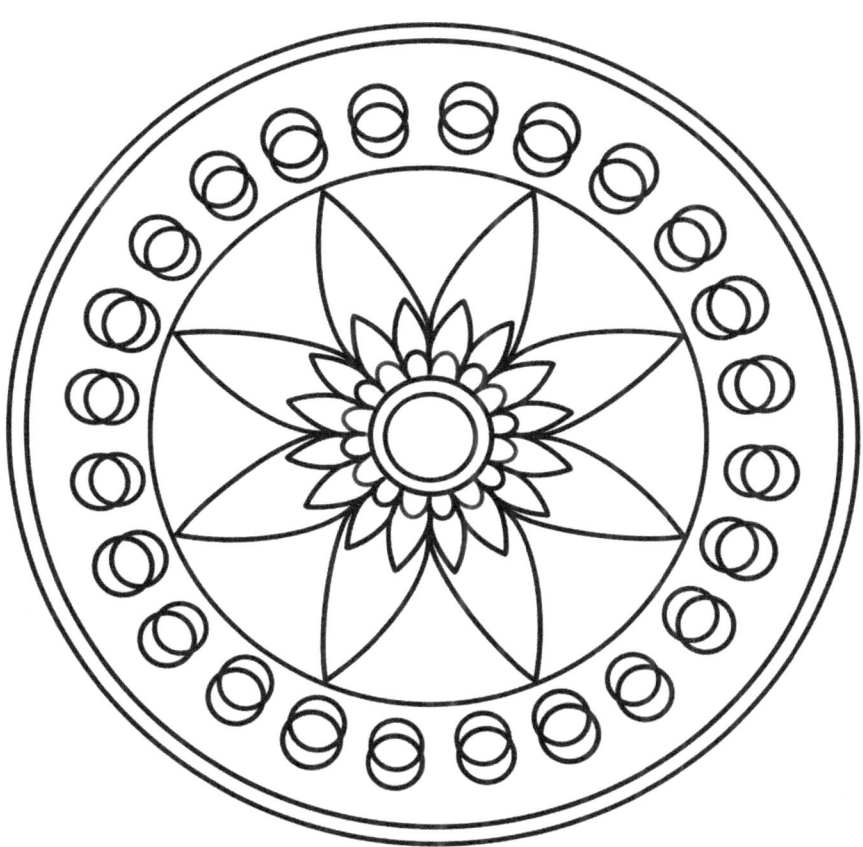

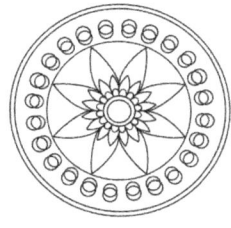 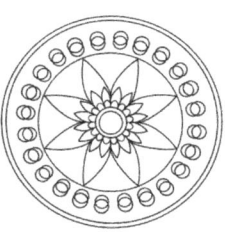 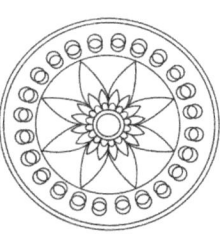 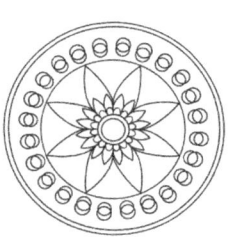 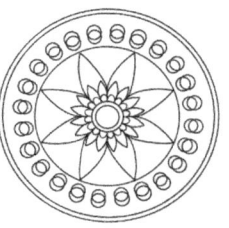

Ans - See!

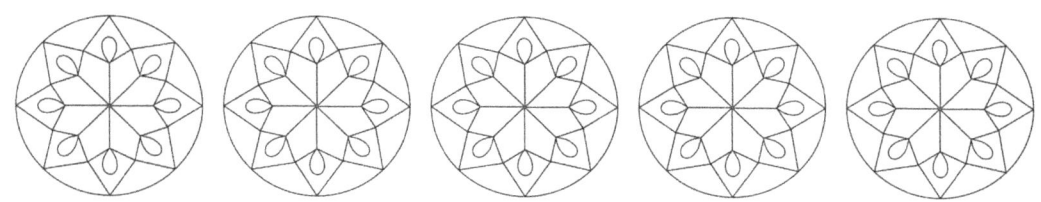
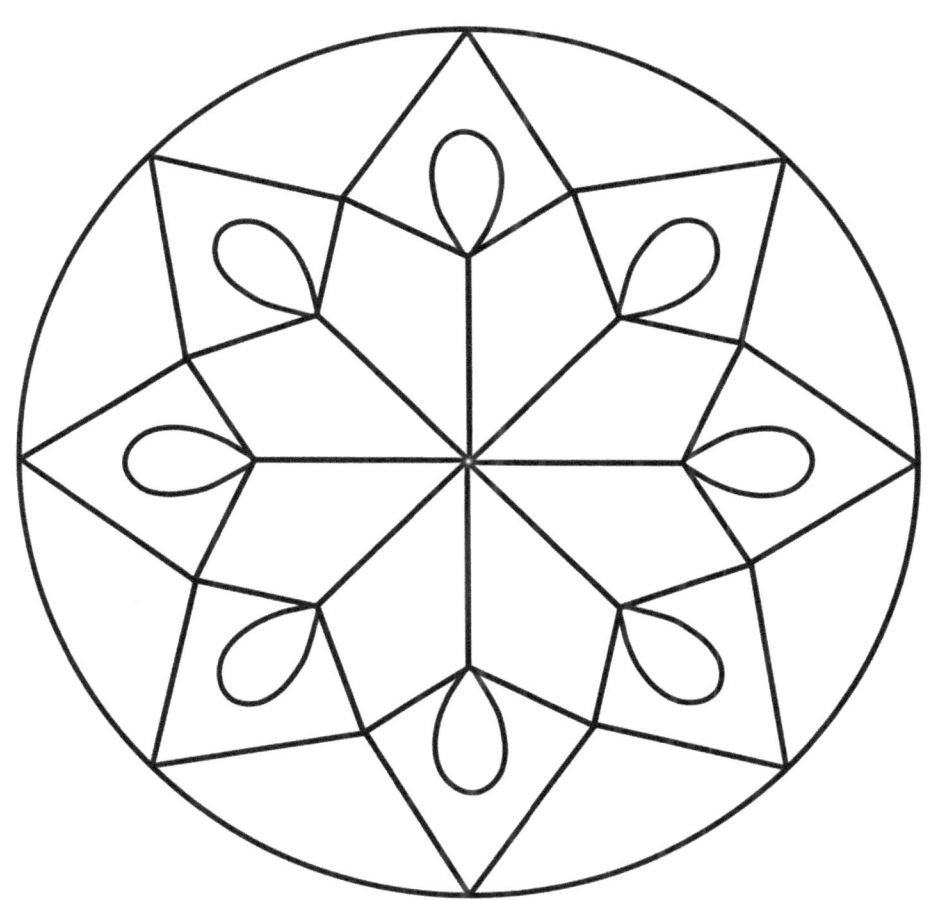
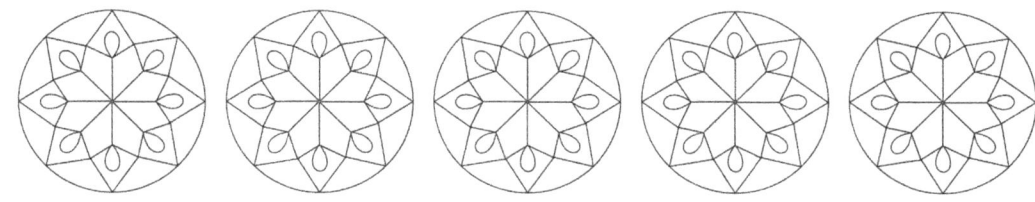

Q - What is a baby frog called?

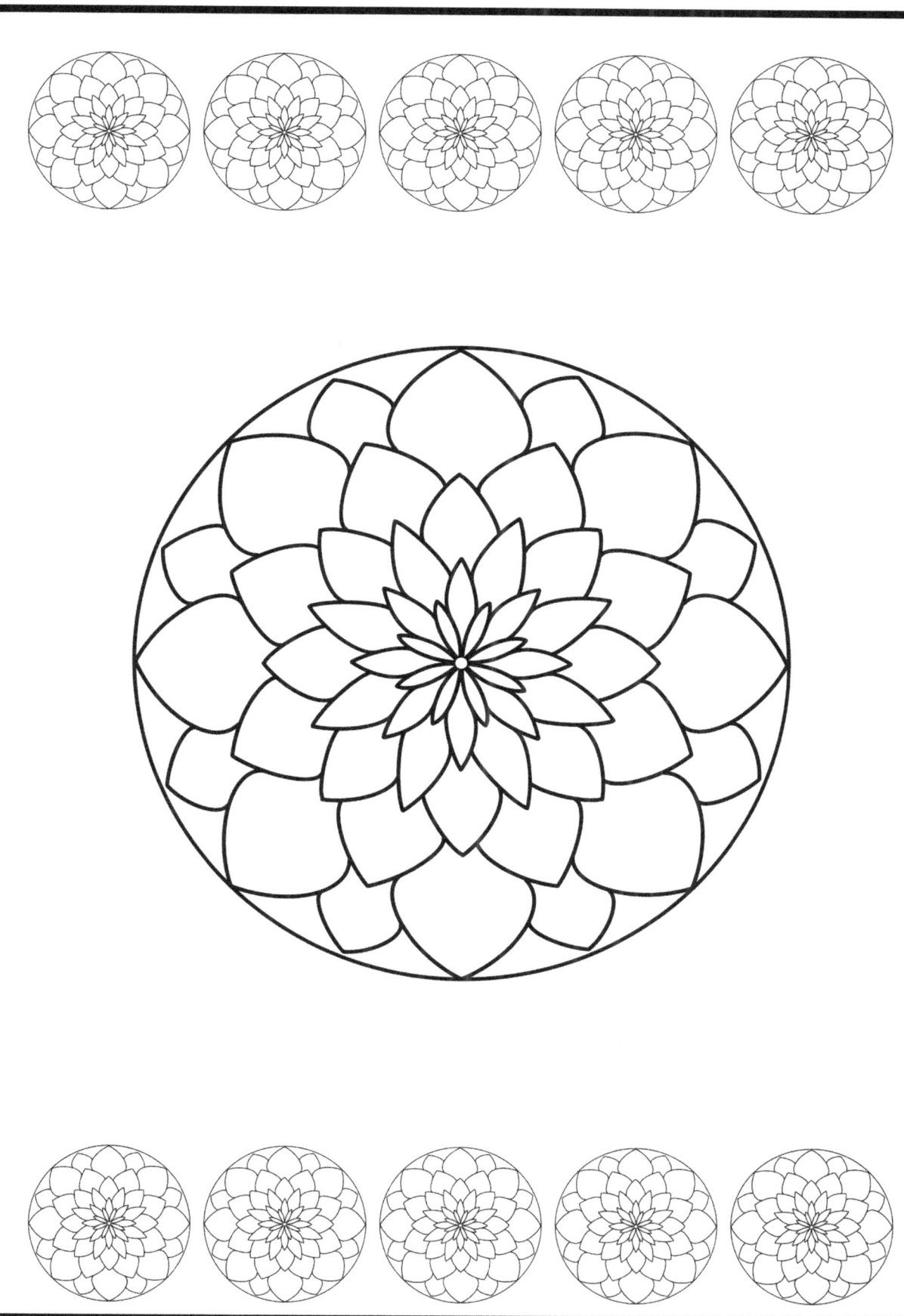

Ans - Tadpole!

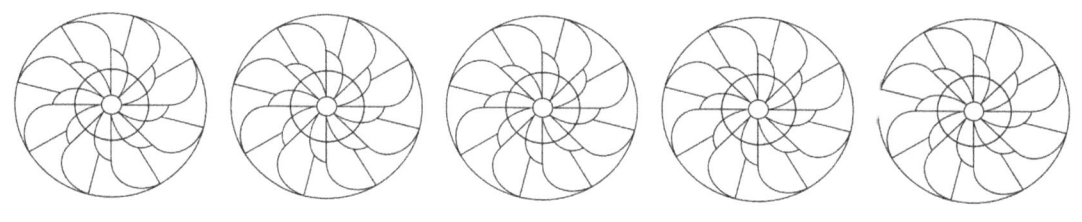
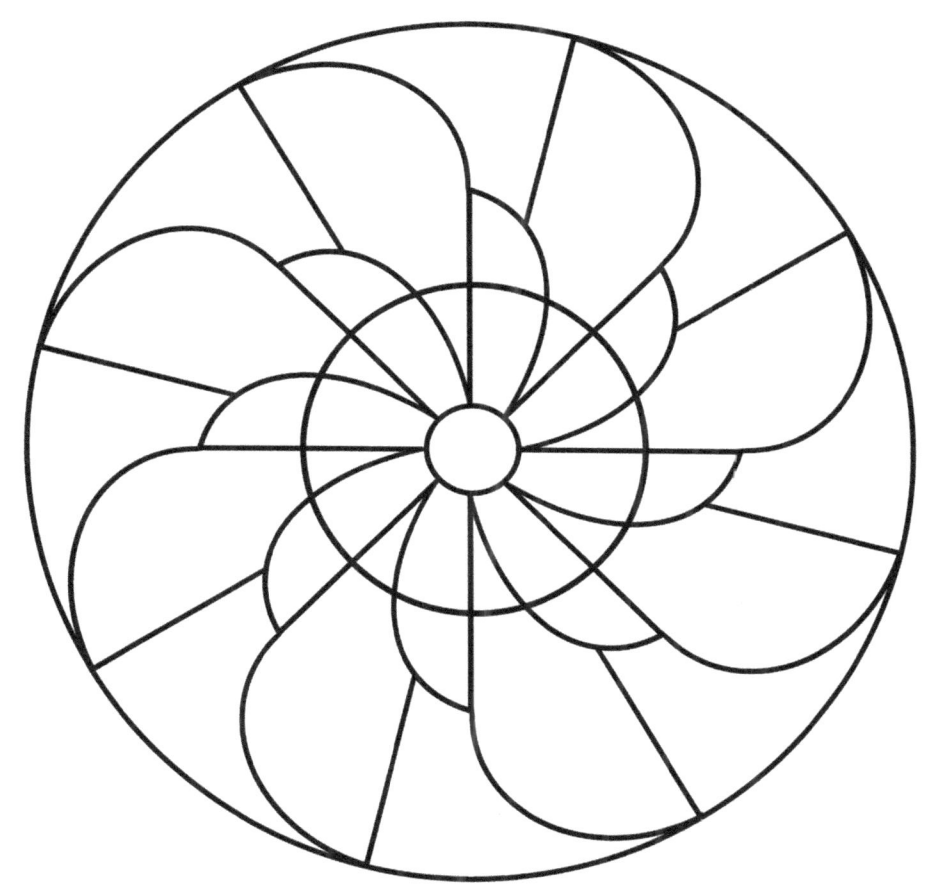
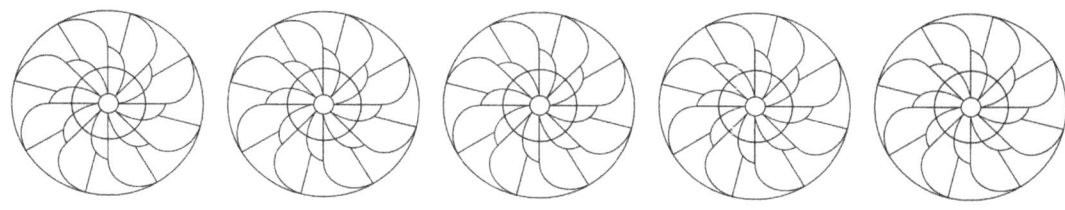

Q - Where does a pig live?

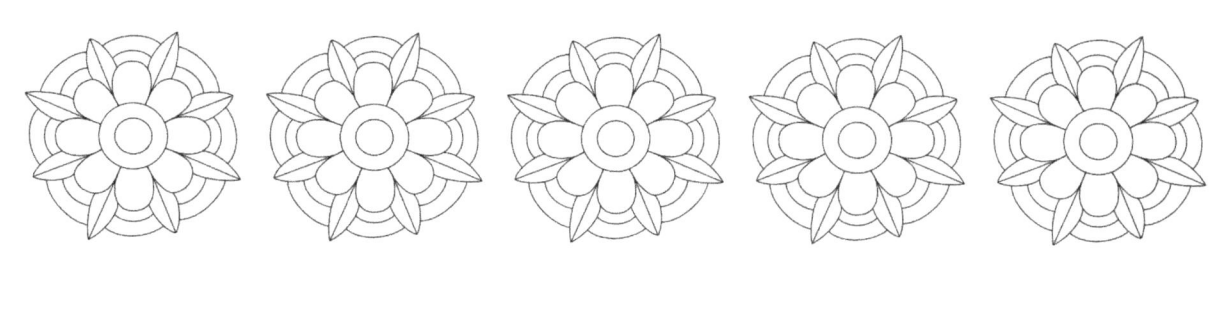
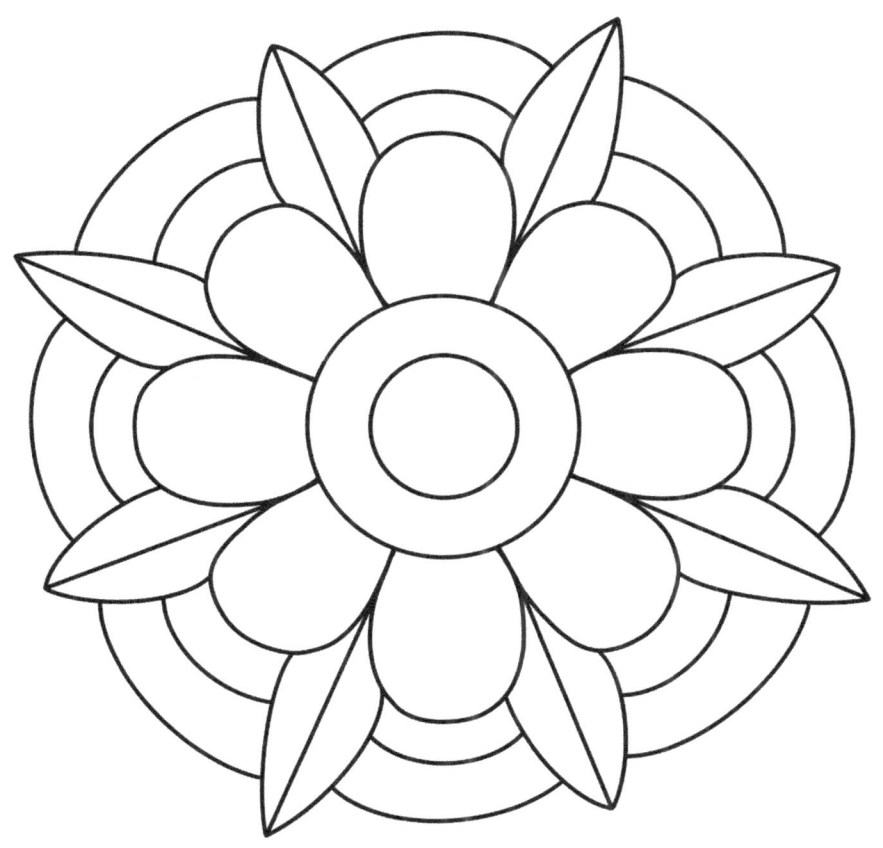
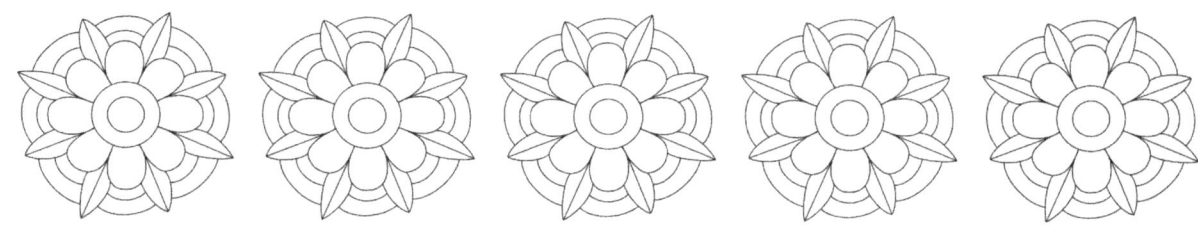

Ans - Sty!

www.ingramcontent.com/pod-product-compliance
Lightning Source LLC
Chambersburg PA
CBHW082020230526
45466CB00022B/2814